Quips and Quotes
For Church Bulletins
E.C. McKenzie

BAKER BOOK HOUSE
Grand Rapids, Michigan

Copyright 1978 by
Baker Book House Company

ISBN: 0-8010-6221-7

Trade edition issued February 1987

Printed in the United States of America

Faultfinding is one talent that ought to be buried.

The Lord giveth if you worketh.

The wages of sin never go unpaid.

Feed your faith—starve your doubts.

Christian charity knows no iron curtain.

There are no degrees of honesty.

Satan has no unemployment problems.

There are too many semi-Christian Christians.

No man has a right to do wrong.

Only you can damage your character.

There is no right way to do a wrong thing.

Doors open for doers.

A PG rating on a movie means *profanity galore.*

He stands best who kneels best.

Choice, not chance, determines destiny.

When tempers flare don't talk—*walk!*

Men with clenched fists can't shake hands.

The person who serves—deserves.

If you must use a hammer, build something.

Salvation is free, but it is not cheap.

Learn to say kind words—nobody resents them.

When a church stops doing, it starts dying.

Tact fails the moment it is noticed.

Show-offs often get showed-up in a show-down.

Enemies are made, not born.

When opportunity knocks, open the door.

Reputation is precious, but character is priceless.

Many a blunt word has a sharp edge.

You cannot prove your religion by its noise.

Money often unmakes the man who makes it.

Truth has bounds; error has none.

Few burdens are heavy when everybody lifts.

Making a sin legal does not make it harmless.

Liquor is trouble put in liquid form.

Common honesty should be more common.

The milk of human kindness never curdles.

You can't win respect by demanding it.

Life is fragile; handle it with prayer.

Behind every schedule someone is running.

Admitting your mistakes is never a mistake.

The most important things in life aren't things.

Sin causes the cup of joy to spring a leak.

Christianity is a battle—not a dream.

The Bread of Life never becomes stale.

Time is but the fringe of eternity.

A person who is self-centered is off-centered

The greatest remedy for anger is delay.

Often small talk comes in large doses.

Blunt people can get to the point quickly.

Nothing is something some folks are good for.

When tempers grow hot, Christianity grows cold.

Never let yesterday use up too much of today.

Prejudice is a loose idea, firmly held.

When embracing opportunity, give it a big hug.

The easiest thing to find is fault.

Formula for failure: Try to please everybody.

Success is sweet, but its secret is sweat.

Knowledge is power only when it is turned on.

To err means you're trying.

Don't entertain ideas—put them to work.

The chief reward for idleness is poverty.

All some people do is grow old.

The best thing not to know is how to give up.

People are as friendly as you are.

Church membership is not an elevator to heaven.

There is nothing busier than an idle rumor.

The man who has a right to boast doesn't have to.

Prosperity makes friends; adversity tries them.

Smiles never go up in price nor down in value.

Living without faith is like living in a fog.

Nothing makes marriage rust like distrust.

God's law lasts longer than those who break it.

Brotherly love is needed as well as motherly love.

It's hard to get ahead if you don't have one.

The religion of many men is in their wives' names.

Hot tempers lead to cool friends.

The know-it-alls have the most to learn.

Sarcasm is usually an insult in dress suit.

Ability is the most important tool in your life.

A pessimist has no starter; an optimist has no brakes.

Why not throw a punch line instead of a punch?

The best thing to save for old age is yourself.

Gossip is what may be called ear pollution.

If you must kill time, be sure it's your own.

A sharp person rarely resorts to blunt statements.

No rewards are offered for finding faults.

Wisdom consists of passing up nonessentials.

Two people can't hate each other if they both love God.

Alcoholic joys are brief—the results are lasting.

Silence is the best and surest way to hide ignorance.

Many people are now trying to find peace in a pill.

Speak kind words and you will hear kind echoes.

Lost hope is the undertaker's best friend.

We can only change the world by changing men.

The trouble with real life is there's no plot.

Man's ears are not made to shut, but his mouth is.

The way to heaven is to turn right and keep straight.

Idleness is the nest in which mischief lays its eggs.

God once shocked the world with a Babe, not a bomb.

Conscience is the referee in the game of life.

If you have a good excuse, don't use it.

Easy Street is still mighty hard to find.

Hats off to the past, coats off to the future.

Charity sees the need, not the cause.

If you fear someone will know it, don't do it.

Those who say the least often say the most.

Some folks are always punctual in being late.

Silence has never yet betrayed anyone.

Nothing is dirt cheap any more except gossip.

Don't beg men to serve—stimulate them.

A homemade friend is better than one you buy.

Give the world what it needs and it will supply yours.

Prayer is not a last extremity; it's a first necessity.

Giving is grace, not disgrace.

Have character, don't be one.

Love covers a multitude of sins—temporarily.

Swallow your pride occasionally. It's nonfattening.

Ideas won't keep. Something must be done about them.

Success is a matter of luck. Ask any failure.

We should forgive and then forget what we have forgiven.

You can *battle* to the top or *bottle* to the bottom.

The best thing to spend on your children is your time.

God called us to play the game, not to keep the score.

Prayer does not need proof; it needs practice.

Many an argument is sound—and only sound.

Poverty is usually the side partner of laziness.

Secret sins won't stay secret very long.

People who do a lot of kneeling don't do much lying.

All the dirt that is spread isn't always in the garden.

Good example has twice the value of good advice.

The right-of-way isn't worth dying for.

Your temper improves the more you don't use it.

Selfishness tarnishes everything it touches.

It is easier to preach ten sermons that it is to live one.

The closed mouth catches no flies.

The silver lining is easier to find in the other fellow's cloud.

Religion is like a wheelbarrow—you have to push it.

The liquor of today is the hangover of tomorrow.

In nature we hear the speech of God.

When at a loss for the right word to say, try silence.

To err is human; to cover it up is, too.

Why not get out on a limb? That's where the fruit is!

The person who stands neutral usually stands for nothing.

It is far better to suffer wrong than to do wrong.

When you think all is lost, the future remains.

The secret ingredient in every recipe for success is *you.*

Freedom is indivisible—it is for all or for none.

No one is too big to be courteous, but some are too small.

Faith with works is a force. Faith without works is a farce.

A sense of humor is the body's best shock absorber.

Most of the time our will power suffers from generator trouble.

The cost of failure is greater than the price of success.

An old hood that never goes out of fashion is falsehood.

If you can't see the bright side, polish the dull side.

A learned fool is more foolish than an ignorant fool.

The fellow with a closed mind usually has an open mouth.

Save energy. God gave us only so much of it.

Grow angry slowly. There's plenty of time.

Impatience has been defined as "waiting in a hurry."

Generally, the criticizer is worse than the criticized.

The most important do-it-yourself project is your life.

Nothing is discussed more and practiced less than prayer.

Learn from other people's mistakes. It's a big time saver.

Nature, time, and patience are the three great physicians.

Some folks seem to have a hard time seeing the obvious.

The lazy aim at nothing and usually hit it.

Never permit anyone to make you so small as to hate them.

There's no diet that will reduce a fat head.

The person who knows everything has a lot to learn.

Some of the most expensive things we've ever had were free.

The Lord loves a cheerful, liberal giver—until he brags about it.

Trouble is always easier to get into than out of.

Enthusiasm is contagious—and so is the lack of it.

Don't let the future scare you. It's just as shaky as you are.

The easiest way to keep a secret is without help.

No one can make you feel inferior without your consent.

If life isn't treating you right, it may be in retaliation.

The university with the biggest enrollment is adversity.

Sometimes the narrowest minds are in the biggest heads.

The Lord loves a cheerful giver; also a grateful receiver.

The good man you can't keep down is probably on the up and up.

Anybody who doesn't make mistakes can't be very busy.

Money separates more friends than it unites.

It's too bad that more people are thoughtless than speechless.

The only time you need pull is when you lack push.

Nobody has ever been bored by someone paying them a compliment.

The fellow who blows his own horn is usually tone-deaf.

It's pretty hard to take a vacation from doing nothing.

Too many people run out of ideas long before they run out of words.

God wants a whole heart but will accept a broken one.

Stretch the truth and your story is going to sound pretty thin.

We have learned how to lengthen life but not how to deepen it.

No life is long enough for a complete education.

A self-made man has no one to blame but himself.

Most entanglements are caused by vocal cords.

Men who do things that count never stop to count them.

Shiftless people seldom get into high gear.

Why look for your ship to come in if you never sent one out?

Being told for our own good seldom does us any.

The wrong way often seems the more reasonable.

Stand up for what you think is right, but be prepared to duck.

An evil eye sees evil things—many times where there is no evil.

Standing on one's dignity can be a mighty small platform.

We all love a good loser—if it isn't us.

You would never recognize some people if they smiled.

Those who live the Christian life never see each other for the last time.

Biscuits and sermons are improved by shortening.

Today's problem is how to stay in the groove without getting in a rut.

Many people don't ignore their conscience. They don't know it that well.

It's better to be a has-been than a never-was.

He who talks constantly is bound to be right—occasionally.

The easiest thing to mind is your neighbor's business.

Sharp words are used by folks with dull minds.

Laughter is a tranquilizer with no side effects.

Giving advice doesn't qualify as charity.

Prayer: "Lord, grant me patience—but hurry up about it."

Everybody wants the same out of life—a little more than they deserve.

Be a self-starter and you won't need a crank to get you going.

Some people have dynamic personalities, while others just explode.

A cheerful countenance has a lot of face value.

The fellow who sits around waiting for a break usually ends up broke.

To belittle is to be little, to be grateful is to be great.

An argument is usually nothing more than audible ignorance.

Step on your stumbling blocks instead of falling over them.

It is sometimes more rewarding to be the giver than the getter.

We are all tied together in the bundle of life.

It's pretty hard to make a come-back for one who's never been anywhere.

Unused experience is a dead loss.

Wisdom is learned from failure much more than from success.

Have you ever noticed how the "I's" of an egotist twinkle?

Too much uplift nowadays is confined to noses.

Facts do not cease to exist just because they are ignored.

Time stays long enough for those who use it.

The superior man blames himself, the inferior man blames others.

Men make counterfeit money and in many cases money makes counterfeit men.

Things are always better somewhere else until you get there.

You can do more good by being good than any other way.

The Bible that is falling apart usually belongs to someone who isn't.

Big ideas can be expressed with little words.

How to dislocate a shoulder: Pat yourself on the back.

You can bank on any friendship where interest is paid.

Always put off until tomorrow what you shouldn't do at all.

Yes and *no* are the traffic signs of your conscience.

Success is doing what you like to do and making a living at it.

Success is a matter of backbone, not wishbone.

Dignity isn't the way you look. It's the way you act.

No dream comes true until we wake up and go to work.

Worry is a merry-go-round, but it rides you.

Don't try to use your influence until you're sure you have it.

Never condemn the judgment of another. You may both be wrong.

A fanatic sticks to his guns whether they're loaded or not.

Don't expect to enjoy life if you keep your milk of human kindness bottled up.

Few people ever carve their way to success with cutting remarks.

If you expect to be praised you'll have to be willing to be criticized.

An egotist never talks about other people.

A real golfer is one who goes to church on Sunday first.

Humor is truth in an intoxicated condition.

The mark of good character should not be left only on tombstones.

Jesus Christ began His ministry at a marriage, not at a funeral.

People who are always in hot water seldom cut much ice.

A lazy man does one thing quickly—he gets tired fast.

You've got the rest of your life to be miserable, so enjoy today.

The best no-fault insurance is to keep your mouth shut.

Profanity is evidence of the lack of a vocabulary—and brains.

Busy folks don't have time to be busybodies.

The finest lessons are learned at mother's knee—and over father's.

Many people quit trying during trying times.

The road to ruin always seems to be in good repair.

No man ever became a failure without his consent and cooperation.

If folks didn't carry gossip, it wouldn't go so far.

An indecisive person wears out the eraser before the pencil.

Bending our knees in prayer helps us from breaking under the load of cares.

Morality, like art, consists in drawing the line somewhere.

When it comes to generosity, some folks stop at nothing.

The more push one has, the less pull he needs.

Tact is the knack of making a point without making an enemy.

The only person who should be happy being down and out is an astronaut.

Say what you will about trouble, it gives you something to talk about.

Life is made up chiefly of foolish questions and unsatisfactory answers.

God's love is available, comforting, abundant, affirmative, and abiding.

Bad men excuse their faults; good men abandon them.

It's a lot easier to grow old than it is to grow up.

The world's most destructive acid seems to come from a sour disposition.

Atheists are really on the spot; they have to sing, "Hummmmm Bless America."

What a man has often blinds people to what he is.

Money doesn't grow on trees; it grows on tries.

Truth hurts. You would, too, if you were kicked around so much.

Don't be sorry if your purse is half empty—be glad it's half full.

Discretion is simply leaving a few things unsaid.

Church is a place where you can meet old friends you never saw before.

A friend in need is usually a friend to feed.

When you have only one thing on your conscience, it's probably a silencer.

A good many things go around in the dark besides Santa Claus.

Flattery has turned more heads than garlic.

Too many things that go without saying aren't left unsaid.

The only thing worse than an active conscience is one that's retroactive.

Anybody who has to ask for advice is probably hard of hearing.

Those who refuse to learn from history are doomed to repeat it.

Never buy anything for a song until you know what the pitch is.

Many people are wallowing in the poverty of their own limited thoughts.

We grow old not by living, but by losing interest in living.

No man is rich enough to buy back his past.

Life does not offer us its best on easy terms.

Rumor is one thing that gets thicker as you spread it.

Modesty is the art of bragging inconspicuously.

Your religion will do more for you if you do more for it.

The man without a country is no worse off than a man without a church.

It is better to understand a little than to misunderstand a lot.

The Bible needs less defense and more practice.

If a fellow can be given hope and confidence, he won't need drugs.

The best level to live on is your level best.

Even hypocrites admire righteousness. That is why they imitate it.

It is impossible to push yourself ahead by patting yourself on the back.

The Lord has as much trouble with soft heads as He does with hard hearts.

Too many people are clamoring for freedom to do what they shouldn't do.

How old do you have to be to be old enough to know better?

Wealth is not only what we have, but what we are.

A church is a hospital for sinners, not a museum for saints.

You put a great deal of pressure on your dignity when you stand on it.

To hatch despair, just brood over your troubles.

Experience is what allows you to recognize a mistake when you have made it again.

Ten years from now, what will you wish you had done now?

Happiness is the art of making a bouquet of those flowers within reach.

The only time some people pray is when they're in the dentist's chair.

Folks who blow their own horn are usually off-key.

Much trouble is caused by our yearnings getting ahead of our earnings.

There's no sadder sight than a young pessimist—unless it's an old pessimist.

We know not *what* the future holds, but we know *who* holds the future.

Few blame themselves until they have exhausted all other possibilities.

Information never gets people into trouble, ignorance does.

You don't have to be much of a musician to toot your own horn.

When a man feels he is utterly helpless, he is.

Arguing about religion is much easier than practicing it.

The world needs a helping hand, not a clenched fist.

It takes some people a long time to get nothing done.

Do unto others as you would have them do unto you, but do it first.

The entrance to trouble is wide; the exits are narrow.

It is unlikely there will ever be a reduction in the wages of sin.

Some Christians go into a summer slump that lasts all winter.

The most unprofitable thing ever manufactured is an excuse.

A flaw in one's character will show up under pressure.

A successful man is a fellow just like you, who worked harder.

Some people change their minds often, and they still don't work any better.

One of the worst mixers to use with vodka is business.

You get plenty of free advice. What you pay for is following it.

Have you noticed that people who aren't smart say things that do?

Running down your friends is the quickest way of running them off.

Too often courage is composed of equal parts of water and bourbon.

If life looks cloudy, maybe the windows of your soul need washing.

By making another's life easier you make your own more worthwhile.

Nothing makes flattery so believable as being flattered.

People who say that certain things drive them to drink should walk.

Love flies out the window when cooing turns to booing.

There's nothing in everyday use so much as tomorrow.

The only thing that can keep on growing without nourishment is an ego.

Life seems full of opportunities for doing what we don't want to do.

Some folks refuse to learn anything they don't already know.

The best kind of fatigue comes from being all-in from going all-out.

Some people have a mouth big enough to sing a duet.

The hardest thing to keep on the track is the train of thought.

Like oil and water, slow hearers and fast talkers don't mix.

Still water and still religion freeze the quickest.

The drunk does not have a drinking problem—he has a stopping problem.

We always agree with people when they admit they're wrong.

It is easier to suppress the first desire than to satisfy all that follow.

Our present energy crisis isn't new. We've been tired for years.

Life is always worthwhile to the person who can laugh, love, and lift.

If you have to be careful about what you say maybe you shouldn't say it.

Progress is where everything takes longer and costs more.

An optimist always sees the brighter side of the other fellow's problem.

Praise is like the fountain of youth. Drink it but don't always believe it.

Spring is the sprouting season, but wild oats grow all year 'round.

Anger, like fire, finally dies out—after leaving a path of destruction.

Gossip is a case of tales and heads both being losers.

It doesn't take much to be too much when you've already had enough.

Pretending to be wise is what makes some people appear so foolish.

Christianity helps us to face the music, even when we don't like the tune.

An egotist thinks there is no satisfactory substitute for himself.

If you can't be a runner-up, try not to be a runner-down.

As a man grows older and wiser, he talks less and says more.

To err is human; to remain in error is stupid.

When you're talking, you're not learning anything.

The man who lives only for himself runs a very small business.

One thing you can give and still keep is your word.

Worry never changes a single thing—except the person who worries.

There may be some new sinners today, but there are no new sins.

The only thing more expensive than an education is ignorance.

Many people need to give their minds a bath.

All truths are equally true but not equally important.

Life begins at forty, but you miss a lot if you wait that long.

A man is never so poorly employed as when he is defending himself.

Compassion is what makes a person feel pain when somebody else hurts.

It's much wiser to choose what you say than to say what you choose.

Chronic worriers often worry about not having something to worry about.

Economics is the art of satisfying infinite wants with limited resources.

You can have 20-20 vision and still be blind to opportunity.

Very few people are fast enough to keep up with their good intentions.

Tact is merely the art of saying nothing when there is nothing to be said.

Praising yourself to the sky is not going to get you there.

A stiff neck usually supports an empty head.

Few speed records are broken when people run from temptation.

He who toots his own horn has everybody dodging him.

Wise men think without talking, fools talk without thinking.

Life makes some people better and others bitter.

Nothing is politically right when it is morally wrong.

Those who have the most to say usually say it with fewest words.

Science has never produced anything as transparent as egotism.

Conscience does not get its guidance from a Gallup poll.

Envy provides the mud that failure throws at success.

There is plenty of heavenly music for those who are tuned in.

Many a man pursues wisdom, but he doesn't always catch up with it.

Laziness is an overwhelming love for physical calm.

A scandal is one thing that has to be bad to be good.

Don't vote a straight ticket unless it is filled with straight men.

The man who never makes an error never plays much ball.

Few people need voice lessons to sing their own praises.

Usually those who deserve least, need it most.

You can preach a better sermon with your life than with your lips.

There's no point in saving wisdom for a rainy day.

Work is a tonic that contains no habit-forming drugs.

Good luck often has the odor of perspiration about it.

A chip on the shoulder indicates there is wood higher up.

People who expect salvation at the eleventh hour often die at ten-thirty.

Acting without thinking is like shooting without aiming.

Zeal without knowledge is the sister of folly.

Almost any system will work if the people behind it will.

Don't lose your head—your brain is in it!

The man who fiddles around seldom gets to lead the orchestra.

Some practice economy only with the truth.

The world has too many cranks and not enough self-starters.

No farmer ever plowed a field by turning it over in his mind.

When you kill time, just remember it has no resurrection.

The world can't be cleaned up with soft soap.

If there is a smile in your heart, your face will show it.

Wrong thinking creates almost every crisis.

Happiness adds and multiplies as we divide it with others.

It's better to make friends fast than to make fast friends.

Never judge a man by his relatives. He did not choose them.

A knocker is like a catfish—all mouth and no brains.

Kind actions begin with kind thoughts.

You can't pass anyone if you stay in a rut.

The person who is all wrapped up in himself is overdressed.

Motivation without knowledge produces fanaticism.

Cars and bars mean stars and scars.

The bigger the head, the smaller the heart.

Those who thirst for knowledge always get it.

As the chest swells, the brain and the heart shrink.

Have courage to let go of the things not worth sticking to.

The church cannot afford the luxury of loafing.

Half-knowledge is worse than ignorance.

Diplomacy is the art of saying nothing nicely.

A good example is the best sermon.

The highway of fear is the shortest route to defeat.

Hatred is cancer of the intellect.

Feel for others—in your pocket!

The one thing certain about life here is that we must leave it.

God promised a safe landing, not smooth sailing.

We need to get God off the charity list and put Him on the payroll.

Defeat never comes to any man until he admits it.

Religion is behavior and not mere belief.

Idle gossip keeps some people very busy.

A person's mind may be broad but have no depth.

We are not punished for our mistakes, but by them.

A wise man will make more opportunities than he finds.

Atheism is not an institution—it is a destitution.

Discipline yourself so others won't have to.

Confessing your sins is no substitute for forsaking them.

Before you criticize a person, walk in his shoes awhile.

It takes a big person to refrain from small remarks.

Friends are made by many acts, but can be lost by one.

Fear falls before the fortress of faith.

What we find depends largely upon what we look for.

You are ahead when you are kicked from behind.

The hardest mountain climbing is getting out of a rut.

Those who pray only when in trouble at least know where to turn for help.

Religious fanaticism is pious bias.

If your troubles are deep seated and long standing, try kneeling.

It is easier to float a rumor than to sink one.

A friend whom you can buy can be bought from you.

The man who loses his head is usually the last one to miss it.

Silence isn't always golden. Sometimes it's guilt.

A Bible in the hand is worth two in the bookcase.

Why not say something funny instead of something nasty?

People seldom notice old clothes if you wear a big smile.

Life's heaviest burden is to have nothing to carry.

A bore never runs out of talk—only out of listeners.

When everybody attends to his own business, news is scarce.

People don't get weak eyes from looking at the bright side of life.

You don't have to institute a lawsuit to collect the wages of sin.

God's biggest problem with laborers in His vineyard is absenteeism.

Some people really enjoy their religion, others just endure it.

Sudden romances usually end the same way.

You can tell when you are on the right road—it's upgrade.

A shady business never produces a sunny life.

It is easier to acquire a good reputation than to lose a bad one.

Conscience warns us as a friend before it punishes us as a judge.

Some people grow under responsibility, while others only swell.

There are no idle rumors. They are all busy.

Crime may not pay, but it sure costs.

A cynic knows the price of everything and the value of nothing.

Idleness travels so slowly that poverty soon overtakes it.

If ignorance is bliss, why aren't there more happy people?

Nothing deflates as fast as a punctured reputation.

People, like refrigerators, need defrosting occasionally.

Be content with what you have, but never with what you are.

No one ever stumbled onto anything worthwhile when sitting down.

The milk of human kindness beats cold cream for wrinkles.

Throwing mud at a good man only soils your own hands.

It's unfortunate that common decency isn't more common.

When you invite trouble, it usually accepts.

As yet, no one has invented a self-starting rumor.

Remorse is often the egg that pleasure laid.

The only way to keep a secret is not to tell it.

The secret of success is still a secret to the average American.

You must arrange in advance for pleasant memories.

Once an opportunity has passed, it cannot be caught.

Conservatism is often merely a polite word for being in a rut.

A lot of people would do right if they thought it was wrong.

Sometimes a reprimand is only a grouch in disguise.

Perpetual peace seems as far removed as perpetual motion.

Jealousy is to the soul what sickness is to the body.

Advice may be had for nothing and is usually worth it.

No man is a successful liar unless someone believes him.

A lot of people waste too much sympathy on themselves.

Some folks lose their religion by letting it escape through their mouths.

Wise men are not always silent, but they know when to be.

Love at first sight deserves a second look.

A chip on the shoulder can become a heavy load.

Spat, spit, and spite are close relatives.

You can't keep your friends if you give them away.

Wearing your halo too tight also gives others a headache.

We live in an age of guided missiles and misguided men.

The way of the transgressor may be hard, but it isn't lonesome.

A rumor is about as hard to unspread as butter.

If revenge is sweet, why does it leave such a bitter taste?

A wayward child is sometimes straightened out by being bent over.

Some people don't think before they speak—nor afterwards.

The lunatic fringe seems to be closing in on us.

Laziness is a quality that prevents people from getting tired.

Some want the benefit of the doubt when there isn't any.

Whiskey has more lovers and fewer friends than anything on earth.

A lie may take care of the present, but it has no future.

All some people learn from their mistakes is to blame them on others.

Never give an excuse that you would not be willing to accept.

Inflation has affected everything except the wages of sin.

Prayer is asking for rain and faith is carrying the umbrella.

Most of us never learn, we just absorb things.

If our faith cannot move mountains, it ought to at least climb them.

Don't blow your whistle so much. The whistle doesn't pull the train.

If at first you don't succeed, you're running about average.

Failure should be our teacher, not our undertaker.

You cannot use your friends and have them too.

The lazier a man is, the more he is going to do tomorrow.

Failure is one thing that can be achieved without effort.

You can judge a man by his enemies as well as by his friends.

So live that when people speak evil of you, no one will believe it.

All people smile in the same language, but not with the same sincerity.

If you must publish someone's faults, publish your own.

True happiness may be sought, thought, or caught—but never bought.

Flattery often corrupts both the receiver and the giver.

You can't believe everything you hear—but you can repeat it.

It is difficult for a man who loses his temper to hold his friends.

The man who thinks he has no faults has at least one.

It's better to know nothing than to know what isn't true.

Gambling is stealing by mutual consent.

Honesty is a question of right and wrong, not a matter of policy.

The folks who know the least know it the loudest.

Friendship is the only cement that will hold the world together.

Confirmed gossipers never gossip about their inferiors. They have none.

Blessed are they who attend strictly to their own business.

A liar is hard not to believe when he says nice things about you.

Conscience is that thing that hurts when everything else feels good.

No man is too big to be kind, but many men are too little.

People seem to be able to stand adversity but not prosperity.

A chronic knocker never goes where he is told to go until he dies.

Drinking to another man's health isn't going to improve your own.

People seldom get dizzy from doing good turns.

A hothead has never been able to set the world on fire.

Piety means letting God bend your will, not just your knees.

A lucky farmer is one who raised a bumper crop of good boys.

The minute you get the idea you're indispensable—you aren't.

If you must make mistakes, make a new one each time.

Few self-made men include humility in their make-up.

So live that when you die the mourners will outnumber the cheering section.

The dangerous age is any time between one and ninety-one.

Most of the stumbling blocks people complain about are under their hats.

One trouble with trouble is that it usually starts out like fun.

Prayer must mean something to us if it is to mean anything to God.

Free advice may prove to be the costliest kind.

It is utterly impossible for any person to demonstrate that there is no God.

There is nothing truly great in man but character.

The best possible thing to do with a debt is to pay it.

Religion is like music, it needs rendition, not defense.

Life is a one-way street, and we are not coming back.

It is extremely difficult to express love with a clenched fist.

Age gives one person wisdom, another grouchiness.

The birth of a baby is God's vote of confidence in the future of man.

There are more warmed-over ideas than hot ones.

Thousands of people are experts on religion but never practice it.

What can't be done by advice can often be done by example.

Whatever your past has been, you have a spotless future.

You never know who's listening, so look before you lip.

The chill winds of adversity may blow off a lot of high hats.

Gossip is like a balloon—it grows bigger with every puff.

You can't live on hope; nor can you live without it.

It is better to be criticized than to be ignored.

Perspiration is the lather of success.

Too many of us are broadminded about the wrong things.

You never lose your reputation; you only change it.

It's later than we think, and most of us aren't thinking.

The most painful wound in the world is a stab of conscience.

Few people are satisfied when they get what they deserve.

It is easy to misconstrue the actions and words of those we dislike.

A good memory is needed once you have lied.

Many folks think that what a church has is for somebody else.

Honest mistakes need correction just as others do.

Tolerance is seeing certain things with your heart instead of your eyes.

Character is like the foundation of a house—below the surface.

There has never been an over-production of kind words.

The heart is happiest that beats for others.

Doubt makes the mountain which faith can move.

Has anyone ever heard of an idle rumor remaining idle?

God's worst has always been better than Satan's best.

The self-made man usually admires his maker.

Love does not keep a ledger of the sins and failures of others.

The person who lives for self alone usually dies that way.

The fellow who knows little soon repeats it.

When one robs another of virtue, he loses his own.

Don't use a gallon of words to express a spoonful of thought.

An open mind and a closed mouth are a winning combination.

The kindness planned for tomorrow doesn't count today.

If you want to convince folks of the value of Christianity, live it.

Better the shoulder to the wheel than the back to the wall.

The Christian life is like an airplane—when you stop you drop.

Many people get unlimited mileage out of a limited vocabulary.

To ignore an insult is the true test of moral courage.

A cynic believes other people are as bad as he is.

Character is not made in a crisis—it is only exhibited.

The longest days are those you start with a grouch.

Religious differences are not as bad as religious indifference.

History records only one indispensable man—Adam.

The fellow who thinks himself a wit is usually half right.

Everybody is liable to make mistakes, but fools practice them.

Nervousness is when you feel in a hurry all over and can't get started.

Wealth makes people admire in you qualities that you don't possess.

He is without humility who sees it in himself.

If money is all you want, money is all that you'll get.

Heaven is a bargain, however great the cost.

A lot of happiness is overlooked because it doesn't cost anything.

Life can be understood backwards, but it must be lived forwards.

To make a success of old age a person must start young.

If some folks lost their reputations they would be lucky.

Prejudice squints when it looks and lies when it talks.

Any fool can criticize, condemn, and complain—and most fools do.

If you must wag your tongue, always make it sound friendly.

You can't go in the wrong direction and arrive at the right destination.

What a man possesses is not as important as what possesses him.

More people worry about the future than prepare for it.

A wave of enthusiasm is seldom a permanent wave.

We often desire most what we ought not to have.

An evil conscience cannot be cured by medicine.

Some Christians have will power; some have won't power.

Death is not a period but a comma in the story of life.

He who gives only when he is asked has waited too long.

An egotist is a person who is his own best friend.

Faith without works is like an automobile without gas.

A cold church, like cold butter, never spreads very well.

It is often the last key on the ring that opens the door.

Some people know how to live everyone's life but their own.

The smile that lights the face will also warm the heart.

Don't try to cheat the Lord and call it economy.

Keep your words soft and sweet. You may have to eat them.

Truth is not only stranger than fiction, but more decent.

It's what we learn after we know it all that really counts.

Some people pray for more things than they are willing to work for.

If a thing will go without saying, let it.

Truth does not need a defender, only an investigator.

A conceited man can walk down Lover's Lane by himself— and enjoy it.

It is seldom as hard to tell the truth as it is to hide it.

Those who live right don't get left.

All parts of the human body get tired eventually—except the tongue.

Many a man has turned and left the dock just before his ship came in.

A lot of opinions which are expressed should have gone by slow freight.

Do what you can, with what you have, where you are.

Those who live in a worry invite death in a hurry.

A person with a closed mind can get by nicely if he also keeps his mouth closed.

Patience is a quality that is most needed when it is exhausted.

To hear some folks talk, what they don't know isn't worth knowing.

Many people nowadays are miracle workers. When they work, it's a miracle.

There are no detours along the straight and narrow path.

Love talked about is easily turned down, but love demonstrated is irresistible.

It is easier to write a guide book to heaven than it is to go there.

Satan is never too busy to rock the cradle of a sleeping Christian.

A braggart is someone who preaches what he practices.

Most of today's news is too true to be good.

We are not punished for our mistakes, but by them.

Success is often just an idea away.

Could you pass an entrance examination for heaven today? If not, why not?

Love's first cousin is trust.

What the world seems to need at the present time is a nuclear balm.

It isn't flattery if you deserve it.

Disappointments should be cremated, not embalmed.

Some folks practice moderation to excess.

In every triumph, there is a lot of TRY.

Sometimes the best applause for children is given with one hand.

Peace is not made in documents, but in the hearts of men.

Now is the time to find out what you've been doing right— and do more of it.

There seems to be no cure for those who are allergic to work.

Be as kind as you can today, because there may be no tomorrow.

We are told that every man has his price, but some hold bargain sales.

The more we count the blessings we have, the less we crave the luxuries we don't have.

Life is what you make it, until somebody comes along and makes it worse.

The Bible never suffers from neglect. It is only those who neglect it who suffer.

Almost everybody is willing to give generously when it comes to advice.

Too often religion is like soap—those who need it most use it least.

You can't lead any farther than you have gone yourself.

Cheer up! Remember that the less you have, the more there is to get.

Real charity doesn't care if it's tax-deductible or not.

The trouble with a lot of childish errors is they are made by adults.

All some people want from life is an unfair advantage.

There are only two ways to be rich: possess much, or be content with little.

The way some people give, you would think the church is coin-operated.

To avoid the risk of losing their religion, a lot of people don't take it to work with them.

We have now reached the point where too many people want to retire before they go to work.

A cold shoulder doesn't attract warm friends.

It may be well to stand tall in this life, but heaven is entered only on the knees.

At death we leave behind all we have and take with us all we are.

Wouldn't it be wonderful if decency would make a comeback so we could read a book again?

If you keep your mind sufficiently open, people will throw a lot of rubbish into it.

As a rule, the wages of sin are unreported.

If you will combine common sense and the Golden Rule, you will have very little bad luck.

The descent to failure is greased with the slime of indifference.

There is no point in crying, "peace, peace," if at the same time we reject the Prince of Peace.

If the Bible is mistaken in telling us from whence we came, how can we trust it to tell us where we are going?

The prayers a man lives on his feet are just as important as those he says on his knees.

Take things as they come—if you can handle them that fast.

The man who really wants to do something worthwhile finds a way; the other kind finds an excuse.

What would the Ten Commandments look like if Moses had been required to run them through a hostile legislature?

A fault recognized is half corrected.

No amount of riches can atone for poverty of character.

Counting time is not as important as making time count.

What the church needs is more men who talk less and do more.

Another difficult problem in the business of life is minding your own.

The man who has strong opinions and says what he thinks is courageous—and friendless.

Wouldn't it be wonderful if we'd all quit drifting and start rowing?

A religion that is not worth exporting is not worth keeping at home.

If you wish to dwell in the house of many mansions, you must make your reservation in advance.

There are a great many ways to go wrong—and a lot of people have tried all of them.

God is in His heaven; all's right with the world. It's just people who have messed things up.

If your religion means much to you, live so it will mean much to others.

How times change! There was a time when people prayed every day and bathed once a week. Now they bathe every day and pray once a week.

There's no heavenly reward for the man who gives away his old overcoat in August.

He who has no Christmas in his heart will never find it under a tree.

Admitting your mistakes is a virtue second only to not making any.

The great use of life is to spend it for something that will outlast it.

There are too many people who would rather hear a good sermon on Sunday than live one through the week.

Conceit may puff a man up, but never props him up.

One thing about wild oats, sowing them is not confined to any one season of the year.

Money does not make a fool of a man, but it does grease the skids if he wants to make a fool of himself.

Sitting and wishing takes just as much time as sitting and planning.

Doing nothing to avoid mistakes is probably the worst one you can make.

Some people spread cheer wherever they don't go.

There's no substitute for a clear conscience, but a bad memory comes close.

The trouble with opportunity is that it usually knocks when we're too busy to open the door.

A man's life, like a gun, can be a blessing or a curse— depending on which way it's aimed.

Satan is perfectly willing for a person to confess Christianity so long as he does not practice it.

Cooking up excuses is no better way of preparing them than dreaming them up.

We ought to treat our elderly people as if we expect to become one of them.

Some people make you think of a river—small at the head, big at the mouth.

There are three kinds of church members: effective, ineffective, and defective.

Generosity will always be a more pleasant memory than stinginess.

He who will not understand your silence will probably not understand your words.

Any recipe for success includes the ability to follow instructions.

Some folks think the statement, "It is more blessed to give than to receive," has reference only to gossip.

One thing about the school of experience is that it will repeat the lesson if you flunk the first time.

There's more hope for a self-confessed sinner than a self-conceited saint.

The Bible has survived the ignorance of its friends and the hatred of its enemies.

Our idea of an agreeable person is a person who agrees with us.

It is well to follow a leader, but wise to see if he is headed in the right direction.

Treasures in heaven are laid up only as treasures on earth are laid down.

Love, like paint, can make things beautiful when you spread it, but it simply dries up when you don't use it.

You're not finished when you're defeated. You're finished when you quit.

Flattery is usually a lie about you told in such a way that you'd like to believe it.

There's no better way to get ahead than by using the one you've got.

An open mind, like an open window, should be equipped with a screen to keep the bugs out.

Prayer will either make a man leave off sinning, or sin will make him leave off praying.

Some people think they need faith as big as a mountain to move a mustard seed.

The worst lies are those that most resemble the truth.

A man's opinions often change—except the one about himself.

Reputation is one of the few things that looks worse when you try to decorate it.

Life's greatest tragedy is to lose God and never miss Him.

A church can't be built with stumbling blocks.

It's a pity more people can't travel the straight and narrow path without becoming straight-laced and narrow-minded.

Learn from everyone—what to do from some, what not to do from others.

Don't laugh at the fallen, there may be slippery places in your own path.

Many people go through life leaning on the complaint counter.

The top of the ladder is a nice place—but terribly lonesome!

Plan ahead. Noah didn't build the ark in the rain.

The world is better or worse for every man who has lived in it.

Most of us would like to have a chance to prove that money can't make us happy.

A marriage may be a holy wedlock or an unholy deadlock.

The meek who inherit the earth will probably contest the will.

Behind every successful man is a pest who wants something.

You can't very well stumble if you are on your knees.

Most of the trouble people get into these days comes through their mouths—either eating, drinking, or talking.

The best things in life are free. Unfortunately, it's not always the best things that we want.

Children who are taught to look up to their elders are seldom looked down on by their peers.

One of our large city churches is planning a skyscraper church building. At least the move is in the right direction.

The man who lives by himself and for himself is likely to be corrupted by the company he keeps.

We would be happier with what we have if we weren't so unhappy about what we don't have.

The man who gets a real good look at Jesus Christ will never be the same man again.

Some people not only expect the worst—they even go out and look for it.

An old-timer is one who remembers when people aimed to get to heaven instead of the moon.

If you will check on the person who says life isn't worth living, you most likely will find that the kind of life he lives isn't.

They have all kinds of new services nowadays. For instance, they've got a dial-a-prayer service for atheists. You dial a number and nobody answers.

Silence may be the best policy, but too many people have allowed their policy to lapse.

You can get into a lot of hot water by blowing off esteem.

A magazine writer recently said we need a new religion. But let's not do anything rash until we try the old one.

Most of the time it is thinking about the load that makes us tired.

Faith is the daring of the soul to go farther than it can see.

When a man says he will do this or that tomorrow, ask him what he did yesterday.

A smile is the carnation in the buttonhole of life.

Happy are they who do not want the things they can't get.

Good days or bad days don't just happen; they're usually made.

The trouble with being sincere is that some people will be inclined to think you're putting on an act.

More than one pessimist got that way by financing an optimist.

If it seems things are going easier, maybe you're headed downhill.

The hardest thing for a person to do is to swallow a dose of his own medicine.

If some people had their lives to live over, they would likely fall in love with themselves again.

Temper is what gets most of us in trouble. Pride is what keeps us there.

Nothing makes it harder to bring up children than being a parent.

A little of the oil of courtesy will save a lot of friction.

A successful man is one who can lay a firm foundation with the bricks others throw at him.

Sometimes those who object to playing "second fiddle" shouldn't be in the orchestra at all.

It's terribly hard to hit your target in life while aiming through someone else's sight.

The Christian life is like a watch—if not wound it will run down.

It may be true that there are no new sins, but folks have sure improved on some of the old ones.

The secret of success in life is for a man to be ready for his opportunity when it comes.

Promises are like snowballs. They are easy to make but hard to keep.

One reason we ought to be more thankful for God's blessings is that we deserve so few of them.

Most of us never lose our tempers. However, we do occasionally mislay them.

The same God who gave us life gave us liberty. Why not make the most of both of them?

Charity is the sterilized milk of human kindness.

Fear is the tax that conscience pays to guilt.

Keep your ideals high enough to inspire you, but low enough to encourage you.

Too many people are ready to give us advice, when what we need is help.

Preachers ought to be as smart as the average washing machine. After it spins dry it shuts off automatically.

The entrances to trouble are wide, and the exits are narrow.

Some want to live only because they are afraid to die.

Little faults can ruin a person, just as little holes can ruin a tire.

People who don't believe in prayer will make an exception when tragedy strikes.

If mankind profits from its mistakes, we have a glorious future coming up.

When you get something for nothing you just haven't been billed for it yet.

The man who takes time to explain all his mistakes has little time left for anything else.

Life is what you make it, or what it makes of you.

A lot of people spend more time placing the blame than rectifying the trouble.

No thoroughly occupied man was ever very miserable.

Going through life is a lot like a football game. You will be forgiven your fumbles as long as you recover them.

Why expect men to unite on religion when they can't unite on anything else?

You have the right to be wrong and hopefully the wisdom to know that you are.

To really enjoy religion, one must have it and then use it.

Money may be a curse, but you can always find someone who is ready to take the curse off of you.

Nothing intoxicates some people like a sip of authority.

Most of us would be in more trouble than we are if all our prayers had been answered.

It is unlikely in the foreseeable future that there will be any serious shortage of ignorance.

Most of us seem to have a natural talent for acting stupid at one time or another.

A person who pours oil on troubled waters today is in big trouble with ecologists.

Care may kill some, but "don't care" kills more.

Revenge is often like biting a dog because the dog bit you.

Too many folks these days are trying to come up with a game plan before they know their way to the ballpark.

Stick to your job until one of you is done.

No one has ever found the hour that was lost.

There would be more geniuses in the world if people retained as much of what they read as of what they eat.

The perfect time to keep your shirt on is when you're hot under the collar.

An old gentleman in Georgia runs a mile every day, saying that when the Lord calls him he wants to be physically fit to make the trip.

People are also judged by the people they keep away from.

Most of us believe it's better not to suffer the morning after than to enjoy the night before.

Nothing is harder for most people to see than the obvious.

You should not pronounce it a poor sermon until you have tested it in practice.

Miracle drugs are nothing new. Moses had two tablets that could cure the world's ills.

To be aware that you are ignorant is a great step to knowledge.

Will someone please step forward and answer the following question: What can we do with out-of-date gossip?

Laughter is to life what salt is to an egg.

If you try to be all things to everyone, you'll wind up being nothing to anyone.

Perhaps this prayer has been prayed many times: "Please, Lord, stop my neighbors from buying things I can't afford."

Some people try to kill time by living it up.

The fellow who can't keep his feet on the ground isn't apt to leave many footprints on the sands of time.

If we got on our knees more often, maybe we wouldn't fall on our faces so much.

We worry too much about shortages and too little about abundances—especially of things like ignorance.

Some folks treat God like a lawyer. They go to Him only when they're in trouble.

Money is like knowledge, the more you have of it, the less you need to brag about it.

The greatest waste in the world is the difference between what we are and what we could become.

A few cocktails help some people to unwind and cause others to unravel.

Many times we may not be able to find help, but there is never a time when we can't give it.

The fellow who always has an ax to grind doesn't cut much ice.

Our journey across the sea of life becomes more pleasant when we scrape off the barnacles of doubt, fear, worry, and pessimism.

The sort of ships that come in while we sit and wait are usually hardships.

A true friend is one who'll tell you what you should know even if it offends you.

The world is full of problem children—and many of them are over twenty-one years of age.

Many people seem to have plenty of speed, but they don't seem to know in what direction they're going.

The way things are now, the study of wildlife should be extended to human beings.

Folks who are always neutral never offend anyone—and never please anyone.

If it were true that we profit by our mistakes, most of us would be a lot wealthier than we are today.

No man ever got to the top of the ladder without friends and fellow-workers steadying it for him.

Any time things seem to be going better, you have probably overlooked something.

This is an age of bargain hunters. If it had been this way in Bible times, we'd probably have been offered another commandment, free, if we accepted the first ten.

The itching sensation that some people mistake for the pangs of ambition is merely inflammation of the wishbone.

Life is getting more complicated all the time. Remember way back when every question had only two sides?

Sticking your nose into other people's business is the surest way of coming face to face with trouble.

The only genius some people seem to have is the ability to destroy what others have built up.

A tactless individual is one who says what everybody else is thinking.

Getting married is like sneezing—even when you feel it coming on you can't stop.

Anybody who thinks there aren't two sides to every argument is probably in one.

Some people go through life getting results while others only get consequences.

The nice thing about meditation is that it makes doing nothing look quite respectable.

When you take responsibility on your shoulders, there isn't much space left for chips.

There is no moral difference between legal and illegal stealing.

Epitaph on the tombstone of an atheist: "Here lies an atheist all dressed up and nowhere to go."

If your trouble is of long standing, try kneeling.

Friendship is like sound health—it's value is seldom known until it is lost.

If you can't tell the difference, what difference does it make?

One trouble with children these days is that they sass back at you even before you say anything.

Some men are slow but sure. Others are just slow.

The difference between a typhoon and a tycoon is in the amount of hot air they generate.

Folks who follow the crowd usually get into a jam.

A handful of Christianity on Monday is worth more than a carload of empty profession on Sunday.

Opportunity does not batter the door off its hinges when it knocks.

Before waiting for your ship to come in, check and see if it ever left drydock!

Character, like embroidery, is made stitch by stitch.

Forbidding prayers in our public schools won't hurt our country as much as forgetting prayers at home.

There is nothing faster than the speed of light. Unless, of course, it's word of mouth.

Where there is no thirst for righteousness, the sermon is always "dry."

Sometimes a "fib" starts out as a little white lie and winds up a double feature in technicolor.

Your temper is a valuable possession, so don't lose it.

Nobody will ever know what you mean by saying, "God is love," unless you act it as well.

The best advice is only as good as the use you make of it.

No one can be caught in places he does not visit.

The people who think they are ahead of the times are merely off the track.

As a general rule, the more one sees of temptation the better it looks.

The best way to appreciate your job is to imagine yourself without it.

Some people have never had anything but experience.

Before you swallow facts, find out who prepared them.

A cynic never sees a good quality in a person but never fails to see a bad one.

Experience is the best teacher because it's on the job twenty-four hours a day.

Most of our faults are more pardonable than the means we use to conceal them.

The father who encourages his son to follow in his footsteps has probably forgotten a few.

There is more need today for common sense than at any time since man stopped having much of it.

Unlike food for the baby, food for the mind is best taken with the mouth shut.

Drivers who think first—last!

The man who has everything probably also has an ulcer.

Life seems to be made up of those who do, those who don't, and those who think they are neutral.

Perhaps the best way to live happily ever after is not to be after too much.

Another measure of civilization's progress is the way the cost of relaxing has gone up.

A sensible prayer: "O Lord, You have given me a mind, and You have given me a mouth. Help me to keep the two connected."

Laughter is the shock absorber that eases the blows of life.

Many people are as lazy as they can afford to be, but not as lazy as they want to be.

The straight and narrow path hasn't developed enough traffic to need a four-lane highway.

Duty is often what we expect of others.

Be grateful for your doors of opportunity and for friends who oil the hinges.

The only joy some people get out of the truth is stretching it.

A good life requires learning, some earning, and some yearning.

The word that's sufficient to the wise is usually enough for the rest of us, too.

Speed may get you to church on time—but they may have to carry you in.

Children are unpredictable. You never know what inconsistency they're going to catch you in next.

Passing the contribution plate is quite different from dropping something into it.

Some freeloaders never turn down an invitation—even when they don't get one.

Better complain occasionally and carry your burdens than cheerfully push them off on someone else.

Why don't we jump at opportunities as quickly as we jump to conclusions?

To know what is right and not do it is almost as bad as doing wrong.

There are many people who are not actually liars, but they keep a respectful distance from the truth.

Those who put on the most style sometimes put off the most creditors.

Revenge may be sweet, but not when you are on the receiving end.

Many a man gets a reputation for being energetic when in truth he is merely fidgety.

We are advised to turn a deaf ear to every scandal, but not many of us have deaf ears.

What chance can a man have to control his destiny when he can't control himself?

The love of money is the root of half the evil in the world, and the lack of money is the root of the other half.

It's give-and-take in this world, with too many people trying to take.

Spilling the salt might be bad luck, but spilling the beans is much more dangerous.

Retirement is when you putter around in the yard and mutter around in the house.

It is with narrow-minded people as with narrow-necked bottles—the less they have in them, the more noise they make in pouring it out.

Silence may be golden, but when there's too much of it between husband and wife it becomes tarnished.

On a church bulletin board in Omaha, Nebraska: "You aren't too bad to come in. You aren't too good to stay out."

It takes exactly three times as long to tell a lie on any subject as it does to tell the truth.

When the other fellow talks that way, it's conceit; when we do, it's honest self-appraisal.

By the time you find greener pastures, you will probably be too old to climb the fence.

The Bible admonishes us to love our neighbors and also to love our enemies. Generally they are the same people.

The world does not pay for what a person knows. But it does pay for what a person does with what he knows.

The moderate drinker does not usually reel when he walks, but he often kills when he drives.

One of the aims of wisdom is to enable one to bear with the stupidity of the ignorant.

Think what others should be like, then start being like that yourself.

In the game of life, one of the most humiliating experiences is to foul out when the bases are loaded.

There is no situation so bad that a few drinks of booze won't make it worse.

It is not the greatness of our troubles, but the littleness of our spirit that causes so much sorrow and heartaches.

You can't hold another fellow down in the ditch unless you stay down there with him.

What is in the well of your heart will show up in the bucket of your speech.

A smile may be your umbrella, but don't save it for a rainy day.

It is easier to raise a storm than to calm one.

You can live here on earth only once, but if you live right, once is enough.

It is neither wise nor safe to trust your business to the man who neglects his own.

The family Bible can easily be passed from generation to generation because it gets so little wear.

People who say what they think would not be so bad if they thought.

Take an interest in the future. That's where you'll spend the rest of your life.

A long face and a broad mind are rarely found under the same hat.

Life's ladder is full of splinters—most of which you don't see until you start sliding down.

Education is learning the difference between wisdom and ignorance and being able to use them both in the right places.

An efficiency expert is usually a person who has no business of his own to wreck.

Actions speak louder than words but not nearly so often.

A lie is a poor substitute for the truth, but the only one discovered so far.

Just because we are entitled to the pursuit of happiness doesn't mean the government should finance the chase.

It's about time folks stopped worrying about what's happening in outer space and start worrying about what's happening in that inner space between their ears.

A good neighbor is one who smiles at you over the back fence but doesn't climb it.

Some people get the point too soon and therefore never learn anything.

A man who trims himself to suit everybody will soon whittle himself away.

Hardening of the heart ages people more quickly than hardening of the arteries.

Some folks think if they wear the best clothes on Sunday they're observing the Sabbath.

The reason parents no longer lead their children in the right direction is because they aren't going that way themselves.

There is a lot of history that isn't fit to repeat.

The world could use more vision and less television.

When in Rome do as the Romans do, that is, if the Romans do as they ought to do.

Liquor is a lubricant only if a man happens to be going downhill.

It's funny how we never get too old to learn some new way to act a fool.

The trouble with being a grouch is that you have to make a new set of friends every few months.

Some people are bent with hard work; others get crooked trying to avoid it.

Freedom not to listen is just as precious a right as freedom of speech.

Men sometimes credit themselves with success and God with their failures.

Home is a place where women work in the absence of men and men rest in the presence of women.

No man has not at some time thought he had most of the elements of greatness in him.

There are a great many more trap doors to failure than there are short cuts to success.

The pleasures of sin are for a season, but its wages are for eternity.

Broken friendships may be patched up, but the patch is likely to show.

It does no good for a person to sit up and take notice if he just keeps on sitting.

There is a growing tendency to play religion on Sunday and play the fool during the week.

The trouble with success is that when your ship comes in, most of your relatives are standing on the dock.

It's a bit difficult to sell a person on a religion you've never lived.

Crime's story would be shorter if the sentences were longer.

When you feel like you ought to explain your conduct, it is a good sign you are doing wrong.

God writes with a pen that never blots, speaks with a tongue that never slips, and acts with a hand that never fails.

There seems to be a problem of children running away from home. It is entirely possible that they are trying to find their parents.

Life is like a grindstone—whether it grinds a man down or polishes him up depends on the kind of stuff he's made of.

It is only at the tree loaded with fruit that people throw stones.

Humility and self-denial are always admired but seldom practiced.

We are living in an age of materialism, but we're running short on material.

A fanatic can't change his opinions and won't change his mind.

Friends are what you think you have oodles of until you happen to need just one.

The nicest people in the world are those who minimize your faults and magnify your virtues.

Gossip is like mud thrown on a clean wall. It may not stick but it always leaves a dirty mark.

If your life is an open book, don't bore your friends by reading out of it.

There would be less juvenile delinquency if parents would lead the way instead of pointing to it.

There is only a thin line between pardonable pride and unpardonable vanity.

Do not condemn the judgment of another because it differs from your own. You may both be wrong.

Gratitude, to many, is an idiotic word. Though it was put in the dictionary, it seldom exists in the human heart.

There are many nerves in the human body, but the most sensitive is the one that goes from the brain to the pocketbook.

The place to be happy is here, the time to be happy is now, the way to be happy is to make others so.

If a fellow loses his key to success, the most likely place to find it is in his work pants.

If the speeches of some men don't reach posterity, it will not be because they weren't long enough.

The price of everything else may go up or down, but the price of success remains steady.

All we are guaranteed is the pursuit of happiness. You have to catch up with it yourself.

The surest sign that a man is not great is when he strives to look that way.

The world does not need a definition of religion as much as it needs a demonstration.

If a person is killed by kindness, the chances are it should come under the heading of accidental death.

People will follow your footsteps more readily than they will follow your advice.

It requires no musical talent to always be harping on something.

God will never allow anything to come your way that you and He cannot handle.

A grouch adds much to the happiness of others by staying away from them.

One reason why there are so many pennies in the church collection is because there is no smaller coin.

Many things history reports weren't worth doing in the first place.

No one can accurately define happiness. You have to be unhappy to understand it.

Knowledge humbles great men, astonishes common men, and puffs up little men.

If we climb high enough up most family trees we are likely to find something hanging there that is not an apple.

Since nearly all sins are expensive, people ought to behave themselves and save the difference.

Never be guilty of judging a man's actions until you know his motives.

When you get the daily bread you have been praying for, do not grumble because it is not cake.

Judging from the general behavior we see in the world today, hell must also be experiencing a population explosion.

In some respects a speech is like a love affair—any fool can start one, but it requires considerable skill to end it.

Nature couldn't make us perfect, so she did the next best thing—she made us blind to our faults.

If swearing, cheating, and cussin' are crimes, then Sunday golf should be abolished.

The tragedy of war is that it uses man's best to do man's worst.

Some people may still have their first dollar, but the man who still has his first friend is really rich.

The trouble with a skeleton in the closet is that it will not stay there.

Every sermon should change the person in the pew, or it should be changed by the preacher in the pulpit.

The reason some people find it difficult to think is that they haven't had any previous experience.

If hard work is the key to success, many folks would rather pick the lock.

The Golden Rule may be old, but it hasn't been used enough to show much signs of wear.

Ulcers are the result of mountain climbing over molehills.

When parents cannot control their children in the home, it is difficult for the government to control them on the streets.

Genuine faith is assuring, insuring, and enduring.

A man with a sense of humor doesn't make a joke out of life; he merely recognizes the ones that are there.

If you were another person, would you like to have yourself for a friend?

Some people don't listen to the voice of conscience because they don't know what channel it's on.

If we had our way we would make good health catching instead of diseases.

Religious freedom is the right of each individual to attend the church of his choice—or go fishing.

You can't depend on your judgment when your imagination is out of focus.

There is still no price war on the milk of human kindness.

Let's not fight for more liberty until we learn to handle what we've got.

Happiness is enjoying what you have instead of fretting over what you don't have.

Genius may have its limits, but stupidity is not thus handicapped.

Medicine and advice are two things more pleasant to give than to receive.

Many people do not entertain evil thoughts—evil thoughts entertain them.

If a man is a liar it is useless to tell him so. He knew it all the time.

They who would not eat forbidden fruit should keep away from the forbidden tree.

Men and sandpaper do their best work if they have a lot of grit.

Life must be worth living. The cost has doubled and we still hang on.

Even if your credit rating isn't very good, you can still borrow trouble.

There are two sciences which every person ought to learn: the science of speech, and the more difficult one of silence.

Another thing that isn't worth what it costs is telling a man what you think of him.

Baloney is flattery laid on so thick it cannot be true, and blarney is flattery laid on so thin we like it.

Some people have eyes that see not and ears that hear not, but there are few who have tongues and talk not.

It is doubtful whether one can be good without being good for something.

The little bird that is always giving away secrets must be a stool pigeon.

You may not be too wise, but if you can manage to keep your mouth shut you can fool a lot of people.

The only time a miser puts his hand in his pocket is during cold weather.

A liar is not believed even when he speaks the truth.

When all the affairs of life are said and done, there is more said than done.

There are very few shade trees on the road to success.

If gambling is a disease, as some claim, could a gambler deduct his losses as medical expenses?

Most people who flee from temptation usually leave a forwarding address.

A religion that won't take you to church services may not be able to take you to heaven.

Never borrow trouble. The interest on the investment is entirely too high for wise investors.

No one knows whether or not a person would be happy if he had all the money he wanted. There isn't that much money.

The best thermometer the year 'round is a warm heart and a cool head.

Among the several things that enable man to be self-satisfied is a poor memory.

The most pleasant fact about the Ten Commandments is that there are only ten of them.

Striking while the iron is hot is all right, but don't strike while the head is hot.

The worst trouble with the future is that it seems to get here quicker than it once did.

It is wise to act wise, unless you are otherwise.

A man's conscience, not his mattress, has most to do with his sleep.

The trouble with most people is that every time they think, they think of themselves.

He who relates the faults of others to you will relate yours to others.

Moderation in sin is no more possible than moderation in hanging.

Something else every married couple should save for their old age is marriage.

Laziness is like money—the more a man has, the more he seems to want.

It's a lot more fun to stop adding up your troubles and turn to counting your blessings.

Almost anything can be bought at a reduced price except lasting satisfaction.

By yielding to temptation one may lose in a moment what it took him a lifetime to gain.

Many people would like to get that wonderful feeling of accomplishment without having to accomplish anything.

Keeping one's mouth shut keeps a lot of ignorance from leaking out.

Wisdom might be defined as having the means to make a fool of yourself and not doing it.

Listen to some talkers and you will then know that practice doesn't always make perfect.

There is no difference between a wise man and a fool when it comes to falling in love.

All of us admire the truth—provided it agrees with our view.

To worry about what we can't help is useless; to worry about what we can help is stupid.

Satan may not be as black as he is painted. In fact, he is more like us than we care to admit.

The loneliest place in the world is the human heart when love is absent.

Too many folks these days expect to go to the Promised Land without making any promises.

Some sermons we hear are a mile long and an inch deep.

Sympathy is two hearts tugging at the same load.

If you can't crown yourself with laurels, you can at least wreathe your face in smiles.

Everyone has a right to do as he pleases so long as he pleases to do right.

A failure is the man who goes through life earning nothing but money.

Faith keeps the man who keeps his faith.

Hard work never hurts some people because they never do any.

Fear makes fools of two kinds of men: the one who is afraid of nothing, and the other who is afraid of everything.

God is in the cleansing business, not the whitewashing business.

Some of us don't know exactly what we want, but we feel sure we don't have it.

Some agile people got that way from dodging the truth.

As scarce as truth is, the supply has always exceeded the demand.

The fellow who is pulling the oars does not have any time to rock the boat.

If silence is golden, not many people can be arrested for hoarding.

Life is just a succession of things to be enjoyed, endured, or licked.

Too many churches have become distribution points for religious aspirin.

Ignorance is like an itch—the less you have of it the better off you are.

No matter how long a person nurses a grudge, it won't get better.

It is sometimes hard to tell whether a red nose is caused by sunshine or moonshine.

Most of us keep one eye on the temptation we pray not to be led into.

After people get what they want they often find they don't want what they've got.

The most important thing a father can do for his children is to love their mother.

When you bury the hatchet, don't bury it in your enemy's back.

The grand essentials to happiness in this life are: something to do, something to love, and something to hope for.

Poverty never drives a man to drink unless he wants to go, but drink will drive a man to poverty whether he wants to go or not.

What every married couple should save for their old age is each other.

To hear truth and not accept it does not nullify truth.

The tragedy of our day is not unanswered prayer but unoffered prayer.

Don't always assume that the other fellow has equal intelligence—he might have more.

After a man makes his mark in the world, a lot of people will come around with erasers.

High octane happiness is a blend of gratitude, service, friendship, and contentment.

All the world is a stage and most of us are desperately under-rehearsed.

A wise man, even when he is silent, says more than a fool when he talks.

Liquor is legal in most places, but some seem to think it is compulsory.

To love and to labor is the sum of life; and yet how many think they are living when they neither love nor labor!

Egotism is the art of seeing things in yourself that others cannot see.

It's almost impossible for people to pat you on the back when you're throwing your weight around.

Tolerance is the patience shown by a wise man when he listens to an ignoramous.

It's a sad religion that is never strong except when the owner is sick.

You can't go around giving someone a piece of your mind without eventually being called empty headed.

All of us intend to be generous—as soon as we have more than we'll need for ourselves.

People who once asked, "Are you married," are now asking, "Are you *still* married?"

We all might enjoy the day more if it started later.

Experience is what enables people to make an old mistake in a new way.

All automobile drivers in favor of saving gas as well as lives, raise your right foot!

Hurricanes and earthquakes are God's way of reminding politicians that they're not really in charge of everything.

Anybody who thinks practice makes perfect doesn't skate on thin ice.

Things turn out best for folks who make the best of the way things turn out.

A good friend is one who thinks you're a good egg, even though you might be slightly cracked.

While hard work never killed anybody, that doesn't seem to be much of an inducement.

As styles change it would be well to keep in mind that it is not the sack, but the potato in it that really counts.

You can always tell an egotist—but unfortunately you can't tell him much.

Everybody likes to hear the truth—when it's spoken about somebody else.

To err is human, to forget, divine.

The best way to find out about your neighbors is to entertain their children.

Jet planes have now passed the speed of sound and will soon dare to approach the speed of gossip.

"Inexcusable mistakes" are made only by the employees. What the boss commits are "justifiable errors."

It's hard to take advice from some people, when obviously they need it more than you do.

The optimist is a fellow who thinks peace comes when a war ends.

You can't forget old friends—they won't let you.

Some countries are like poorly planned cocktail parties—too many people, too little food.

It's likely that children would never dream of doing many things if they weren't told to—or not to.

Some nest eggs nowadays are becoming dehydrated.

There are two kinds of people in your church: those who agree with you and the bigots.

A truly religious person is one who prays often even if he doesn't want anything.

This would be a far nicer world if antique people were valued as highly as antique furniture.

The hardest job that church members have is to move their religion from their throats to their muscles.

In a man's circle of friends there are sometimes triangles which should encourage him to remain square.

Find some good in everybody, and perhaps everybody will find some good in you.

Genius is simply the ability to avoid extra work by doing it right the first time.

First, we get all the facts possible. Then, usually, we distort them to suit whatever argument we're involved in.

One good thing about being poor is that you don't panic over the stock market.

The love of money is the root of evil, except now money isn't around long enough for even a fleeting romance.

Be courteous to everybody and you'll confuse them. They'll probably think you haven't anything important to do.

Sometimes a man must protest, not to change the world, but to keep the world from changing him.

Before you flare up at anyone's faults, take time to count ten—ten of your own.

The tragedy of men is often not so much in what happens to them as in what they are missing.

Nothing helps you to keep your chin up as much as not being afraid to stick it out.

Driving a car is like baseball—it's the number of times you reach home safely that counts.

In times like these it helps to remember that there have *always* been times like these.

Society is not wise enough to see the power of sin or religious enough to see the guilt of sin, but it cannot fail to see the stain of it.

Have you noticed that some folks get into deep water trying to make a big splash?

Few people want more than their share, but many have an exaggerated idea of what their fair share is.

One moment of patience may ward off a great disaster; one moment of impatience may ruin a whole life.

Nowadays if you're offered the world on a silver platter, don't be foolish—take the platter.

A lot of history is usually just gossip that has become respectable with age.

One trouble with our economy is that it's hard to find a man who's willing to work for what he's worth.

If the Lord had really created all men equal, we wouldn't need both the long form and the short form.

Kids are people who spread happiness, peanut butter, and measles.

Most misfortunes are easier to bear than the fear of those that haven't happened—and probably never will.

It's easy to recognize a man of virtue. He's the one who always does right even when nobody's looking.

A successful person is one who went ahead and did the things the rest of us never quite got around to.

The person who said talk is cheap never hired a lawyer.

If a bore had invented the telephone, nobody would have answered his call.

Some folks are like Easter eggs—ornamented on the outside and hardboiled on the inside.

People who always bend over backward to please everybody soon weaken their spine.

There are some days when the only things that come off on schedule are your shirt buttons.

Small children seem to be afflicted as much as ever with whatever it is that prevents them from being sleepy at bedtime.

He who is miserly will do right when he finds it cheaper to do so.

Remember the good old days when you had to do without some things because you couldn't afford them? They're back!

To profit from your mistakes if you don't have any, you have to go out and make some.

We like for a man to say what he thinks—that is, when he agrees with us.

Advice to some folks is about as welcome as a bumblebee in the bathroom.

If something goes wrong, it is more important to decide who is going to fix it than who is to blame.

Once we thought the world was flat, then round. Now we know a lot of it is crooked.

A genius is a guy who solves a problem you didn't know you had, in a manner you don't understand.

It's easy to have a happy personality. Just forget your troubles as easily as you forget your blessings.

Egotism is obesity of the head.

Sign on a church bulletin board in Atlanta, Georgia: "Don't keep the faith—spread it."

Those who imagine the world is against them have generally conspired to make it true.

If more people would abide by the tablets brought down by Moses from Mount Sinai, they'd need fewer tablets from the drug store.

The wishbone will never replace the backbone.

We're not sure which worries us most—the end of the world or the end of the month.

There's always an easy solution to every human problem—neat, plausible, and wrong.

Resisting temptation is usually just a matter of putting it off until nobody's looking.

Cocktail parties are where some of the best reputations are dissolved in alcohol.

No man or woman becomes experienced all at once—except when falling in love.

Tomorrow will simply be an extension of today, and likely won't be any better or worse than today unless we make it so.

One of the hardest things to take and one of the easiest things to give is criticism.

A bore is someone who doesn't have much to say, but you have to listen a long time to find out.

Seat belts cost less than the windshields they keep you from going through.

The best things in life are free. It's the worst things that are so expensive.

More people would learn from their mistakes if they weren't so busy denying they made them.

A lot of folks get credit for being patient, when the truth is that they don't have the nerve to start anything.

The world is short on scholars but long on authorities and experts.

We can often do more for other people by correcting our own faults than by trying to correct theirs.

A recent survey shows there are more people asking questions than answering them.

Some of the new movies don't need wider screens—the theaters need wider exits.

The best time to end your speech is before you planned to.

Anybody who is always raising the roof probably doesn't have much in his attic.

It's all right to save money, but too many are trying to save it from people they owe it to.

No matter how small your vocabulary is, it's still big enough to let you say something you'll later regret.

The important time to keep on trying is when you reach the point where the average person would quit.

There is nothing as disastrous as embarking on the sea of matrimony with the wrong dreamboat.

Failure always follows the path of least persistence.

The conversations Adam and Eve had must have been difficult at times—they had nobody to talk about.

Tact is the art of recognizing when to be big and when not to belittle.

The largest thing in the smallest container is common sense in a human head.

A man who lives a double life often gets through it in half the time.

Some people are so suspicious that they wonder what you mean when you ask them how they are getting along.

If anything more happens it will be at least six months before we will have the time to worry about it.

Early to bed, early to rise, enables you to save enough to do otherwise.

You just can't expect opportunity to knock in a country that knocks opportunity.

A well-adjusted person is one who makes the same mistake twice without getting nervous about it.

It's easy for most of us to see how to cure our problems, but hard to accept the cure.

Advertising and matrimony have something in common—both tend to make people live beyond their income.

It's doubtful if the largest telescope will ever be able to pick up what some men apparently see through a glass of whiskey.

The stock market tape often gets more people in trouble than the Watergate tapes.

You're never quite sure what kind of a mind anybody has until you are given a piece of it.

The average number of times some people say no to a temptation is once—weekly.

When a preacher rehearses his Sunday sermon, you could say he is practicing what he preaches.

The trouble with the school of experience is that the course is so long that the graduates are too old to go to work.

It would be a happier world if complaints came only from folks who had something to complain about.

We are now living in a machine age. The only thing people are doing by hand these days is scratching themselves.

A person who talks a lot will occasionally say something worthwhile—but the chances are no one will be listening.

No one really thinks he's better than anybody else. He just wants to be treated that way.

Life for most of us is a continuous process of getting used to things we hadn't expected.

Most of us are quick to recognize a good thing the minute the other fellow sees it first.

To know things as they are is better than to believe things as they seem.

A smile will go a long way if you give it a good start.

The new computers do almost everything but think—which makes them almost human.

There's no point in burying the hatchet if you're going to put up a marker on the site.

If you kicked the person who caused most of your troubles, you probably couldn't sit down for two weeks!

He who believes that all things come to him who waits hasn't waited very long.

It's not advisable to tell everything you know, but it's best to know everything you tell.

History is always repeating itself. Every country seems ready to go into a bloody war to prove how much it wants peace.

How to keep your marriage from falling apart: Whenever you're wrong, admit it, and whenever you're right, shut up.

Some folks don't have time to talk about their religion—they're too busy living it.

Public opinion pollsters say 8 percent of the public has no opinion. Why don't we ever meet any of these pleasant people?

Logic is nothing more than rearranging the facts to justify your confusions.

Many a kid grows up thinking a switch hitter is a parent.

All types of people make up our world: right-handed, left-handed, and under-handed.

With all the trouble in the world today, if the pessimists aren't satisfied now they never will be.

Most of us are too fast on the draw. If our mouths were guns we would kill a lot of innocent people.

It's difficult, if not impossible, to get along with folks who have a "Do not disturb" sign on their opinions.

Asking your advice is what gives a lot of folks an opportunity to tell you where you're wrong.

If nobody is standing in your way, you must be on the wrong track.

There's nothing you're more apt to strain in patting yourself on the back than somebody else's patience.

Life's necessities have increased to four: food, clothing, shelter, and endurance.

Bores can be divided into two classes—those who have their own particular subject and those who don't need a subject.

When you come to the end of a perfect day, perhaps you'd better check back carefully.

Some people buy their way out of trouble, but even more have bought their way into it.

If a fellow isn't thankful for what he's got, he isn't likely to be thankful for what he's going to get.

Did you hear about the man who decided to procrastinate? He never got around to it.

It is wise to hold back on the tongue what never should have been on it in the first place.

A skeptic is a fellow who doesn't believe anything he reads and only half of what he says.

Anybody who thinks practice makes perfect doesn't have a child taking saxophone lessons.

Isn't it amazing that we have managed to survive to this point, only to have the younger generation tell us how wrong we have been?

You're wrong if you think the best way to solve a problem is to talk it to death.

Some folks don't let their right hand know what their left hand is doing because they don't want to embarrass their right hand.

The man who quits smoking cigarettes never forgets the day he stopped—or lets anyone else forget it, either.

Many a man expects his wife to be perfect and to understand why he isn't.

Playing second fiddle is a great deal better than being left out of the orchestra.

One thing you can get more of for your money these days is less.

Failure is more often the result of a lack of energy than a lack of capital.

To some people a mixed marriage is when two people marry outside their astrological sign.

Blessed is the man who, having nothing to say, abstains from giving us wordy evidence of the fact.

In managing your money you should be tight enough to be economical and loose enough to be charitable.

After all, life is quite simple. We are the ones who usually create the circumstances that complicate it.

The same man who rarely hears the shrill voice of conscience never misses the whisper of temptation.

A fool who is soon parted from his money is hard to detect among the rest of us having the same problem.

Good advice may be more valuable than money, but most people prefer cash.

A successful marriage is built on common trust and an occasional compliment.

Some folks get so low and good-for-nothing that they have to reach up to touch bottom.

Judge each day not by the harvest you reap but by the seeds you plant.

The greatest danger to free speech is that many people who have it are too free with it.

A lot of folks go well beyond the call of duty to get even farther away from it.

Did you ever notice how your belief in heredity is reinforced when one of your children does something outstanding?

You're never going to get anywhere if you think you are already there.

The key to almost everything is patience. You get the chicken by hatching the egg, not by smashing it.

It takes courage to stand up and be counted, but to keep on standing up after being counted is the real test.

When you borrow money from a friend, think first of which of the two you need most.

Many people are like icebergs—wherever they go they lower the temperature.

Most people like to do important things if it's not too much work, if the responsibility is not too great, and if they can get their picture in the paper.

You never really get old—what happens is that you suffer from a youth deficiency.

It's embarrassing to make a mistake, but it's more embarrassing to find out you're so unimportant that nobody noticed it.

Motto displayed over the desk of a country editor: "Lord, give me this day my daily idea, and forgive me the one I had yesterday."

It is a curious world in which a man can be blowing his own horn and playing second fiddle at the same time.

Every time dishonesty wins it gets harder to convince kids that honesty is the best policy.

Have you ever noticed the depths to which some people will descend to reach the heights?

It's about time women began taking over the world. It sure could use some mending.

The number of idle workers in this country would be much greater if those who have jobs were included.

A man's life is like a piece of metal—it can be forged into a tool to aid him or a weapon to destroy him.

The trouble with burying the hatchet is that the other fellow usually has a map of just where.

Perhaps those "Saturday Night Specials" wouldn't present such a problem if we had more Sunday morning regulars.

Learning to speak in two languages is not nearly as hard as learning to keep your mouth shut in one.

Bringing up children is always more successful when they are reared now and then with a paddle.

A good imagination is what enables one to enjoy the good times that never happened.

Try living within your income and you'll live without worries—and also without a lot of other things.

Many people believe in luck. How else can you explain the success of those you don't like?

A farmer once said his mule was awfully backward about going forward. This is also true of many human beings.

Character is not the only thing in life, but it is far ahead of whatever is in second place.

Being put on a pedestal is all very fine and good as long as you keep your feet on the ground.

The safest way to cross the street is without being hit.

Anyone nowadays who plugs into current affairs is bound to get shocked.

There may be something wrong with our swallowers because we choke on some of the things we are expected to swallow.

The aim of some men is to have peace in the world. Others would settle for peace in the family.

In diagnosing the illness of modern society, many are willing to write the prescription but few are willing to take the medicine.

One trouble with a lot of folks is that they are more interested in speed than in direction.

A man in Montana complained, "Things just aren't what they used to be—and one of them is me."

If society gets to the point where there is a job for everybody, a lot of folks are going to be unhappy.

You may think that liquor peps you up, but in the end it lets you down.

The thing that makes it tough to find fault with some people's work is that they seldom do any.

Few things are as hard to use in moderation as a comfortable rocking chair.

The money a fool is soon parted from probably won't stay with anybody else very long either.

It's not the ups and downs of life that bother the average man. It's the jerks.

Security is dangerous when you are confident you have all that you need.

It's a shame that a mirror doesn't make some people see themselves as others see them.

Many of us believe in the hereafter. What we find hard to believe in is the here and now.

We often wonder how much pollution is caused by people airing their grievances.

If silence is the beginning of wisdom, some people never made it through kindergarten.

Truth will win every argument if you stick to it long enough.

You can make more friends in two months by becoming interested in people than you can make in two years trying to get people interested in you.

It is in leisure time that men are made or marred.

Good leaders are now so scarce that many people are just following themselves.

A Christian shows what he is by what he does with what he has.

Good ideas need landing gear as well as wings.

Never carry your knowledge or your shotgun at half cock.

Many good resolutions start too late and end too soon.

Borrowing neighbors usually take anything but a hint.

Nothing makes it harder to find a hiding place than having children.

Four reasons for not drinking booze: the head is clearer, the health is better, the heart is lighter, and the purse is heavier.

Your promises to God should be as binding as those to the bank.

Nobody has yet listened himself out of a job.

The worst use you can make of success is to boast of it.

Fast, reckless driving often leads to slow, soft music.

Along with everything else, the facilities for getting into trouble have been improved.

Many a public speaker who rises to the occasion stands too long.

It would have been better for some self-made men if the job had been done by someone else.